Table of Contents

INTRODUCTION

Baked beans are an international food. Versions of baked beans are found across the globe from France, home of the cassoulet, through to the USA where Boston baked beans rein

Despite being called "baked" beans, they are most commonly stewed in a tomato sauce. Canned baked beans are usually made from haricot beans, also known as navy beans.

What are baked beans

Baked beans are a stable store cupboard ingredient of beans in a rich and tasty tomato sauce. They can usually be bought in a tin from the supermarket.

Why baked beans are healthy

• A cup of baked beans is a great source of protein with more than 10 grams of protein equal to 50 gram steak or 1 1/2 eggs.

• Baked beans contain energy giving, low glycaemic index carbohydrates.

• Baked Beans count as a vegetable serve. A cup of baked beans is equal to more than 1.5 serves of vegetables.

• Most baked beans are also an excellent source of tomato containing the antioxidant lycopene.

• Baked beans contain folate a vitamin essential to release the energy in our food. One cup of Baked Beans provides more than 25% of the daily requirement (RDI 400 micrograms/day adults and teenagers).

• The fibre in a cup of baked beans is 12 grams equal to more than 8 large sandwich slices multigrain bread, or 1 1/4 cups toasted muesli or 4 medium unpeeled green apples.

What type of beans are baked beans?

With so many different types of beans available, if you've ever wondered what kind of beans are in a tin of baked beans, you're not alone.

Baked beans are made using a type of haricot beans known as navy beans.

How many beans are in a can of baked beans?

On average, there are approximately 465 beans per standard 415g can of beans.

Different types of beans

Did you know there are 400 different varieties of beans? Here are just a few of them...

• Black Beans - A staple in many Mexican and Brazilian dishes, these beans have a velvety-smooth texture and mild flavour.

• Cannellini Beans - Also known as white Italian kidney beans, these cream-coloured beans are one of the most common types of beans and are a popular addition to soups and salads,

• Kidney Beans - Recognised by their vibrant red skin and white interior, kidney beans have a mild flavour and make a great addition to any chilli recipe.

• Chickpeas - There are two varieties of chickpeas: kabuli and desi. With a round shape and a firm texture, you're probably familiar with them because they're used to make hummus.

• Edamame - These young soybeans re usually eaten while still inside the pod. These beans are soft and edible, unlike mature soybeans.

Recipes

Boston Baked Beans

Baked beans are the perfect addition to any outdoor cookout or barbecue. These baked beans are slow-cooked in the oven with bacon, onions, and a sweet, syrupy sauce, resulting in an old-fashioned taste that everyone will enjoy. This easy recipe has been served by my family for over 29 years and originally came from my mother-in-law. It tastes great served with fresh cornbread or biscuits and honey.

Ingredients

- 2 cups dry navy beans, soaked overnight

- ½ pound uncooked bacon strips

- 1 medium onion, diced

- ½ cup ketchup

- 3 tablespoons molasses

- ¼ cup brown sugar

- 1 tablespoon Worcestershire sauce

- 2 teaspoons salt

- ¼ teaspoon ground black pepper

- ¼ teaspoon dry mustard

Directions

- Transfer soaked navy beans and soaking water to a saucepan; bring to a boil. Reduce heat and simmer until tender, approximately 1 to 2 hours. Drain and reserve the cooking liquid.

- Preheat the oven to 325 degrees F (165 degrees C).

- Arrange 1/2 of the beans in the bottom of a 2-quart casserole dish. Place 1/2 of the bacon strips over the beans and sprinkle 1/2 of the onions over top. Repeat layers once more.

• Combine ketchup, molasses, brown sugar, Worcestershire sauce, salt, pepper, and dry mustard in a large saucepan over medium heat; bring to a boil.

• Pour sauce over the beans. Pour in just enough reserved cooking liquid to cover the beans. Cover the casserole dish with a lid or aluminum foil.

• Bake in the preheated oven for 1 1/2 hours. Remove the lid and continue to cook, checking every 1/2 hour or so and adding more cooking liquid if necessary to prevent the beans from getting too dry, until beans are tender, 1 1/2 to 2 1/2 more hours.

Baked Beans from Scratch

Ingredients

• 1 cup navy beans, soaked overnight and drained

• 4 cups water

• ¼ cup ketchup

• ¼ cup maple syrup

• 2 tablespoons brown sugar

• 2 tablespoons molasses

• 1 teaspoon Worcestershire sauce

• ½ teaspoon salt

- ⅛ teaspoon ground black pepper

- ⅛ teaspoon chili powder

- 1 small onion, chopped

Directions

- Place beans in a large saucepan with 4 cups of water. Bring to a boil over high heat, then reduce heat to medium-low, cover, and simmer 1 hour.

- Preheat the oven to 375 degrees F (190 degrees C). Stir ketchup, maple syrup, brown sugar, molasses, Worcestershire sauce, salt, pepper, and chili powder together in a small bowl; set aside.

- Once beans have simmered for 1 hour, drain, and reserve cooking liquid. Pour beans into a 1 1/2-quart casserole dish; stir in chopped onion and molasses mixture. Stir in enough reserved cooking liquid so sauce covers beans by 1/4 inch.

- Cover and bake in the preheated oven for 10 minutes; reduce heat to 200 degrees F (95 degrees C) and cook 6 hours longer, stirring beans after they have cooked for 3 hours. Once beans are tender and sauce has reduced and is sticky, remove from the oven, stir, recover, and allow to stand 15 minutes before serving.

Simple Baked Beans
Ingredients

• cooking spray

• 2 (16 ounce) cans baked beans with pork

• ¼ cup molasses

• ¼ cup chopped onions

• 4 tablespoons brown sugar

• 2 tablespoons ketchup

• 1 tablespoon prepared mustard

• 2 slices bacon, chopped

Directions

• Preheat the oven to 350 degrees F (175 degrees C). Grease a casserole dish with cooking spray.

• Mix together baked beans with pork, molasses, onions, brown sugar, ketchup, and mustard together in a large bowl. Transfer mixture to the prepared dish and top with chopped bacon.

• Cover and bake in the preheated oven until thickened, about 3 hours.

Slow Cooker Homemade Beans

These slow cooker beans are especially great for football Sundays or frozen for a later occasion. A delicious recipe for homemade beans that can be served as a main course or as a side dish.

Ingredients

• 3 cups dry navy beans, soaked overnight or boiled for one hour

• 6 slices thick cut bacon, cut into 1 inch pieces

• 1 large onion, chopped

• 1 ½ cups ketchup

• 1 ½ cups water

• 1 cup brown sugar

• ¼ cup molasses

• 1 tablespoon dry mustard

• 1 tablespoon salt

Direction

• Drain soaking liquid from beans; place them in a slow cooker.

• Stir bacon, onion, ketchup, water, brown sugar, molasses, mustard, and salt into beans until well mixed.

• Cover and cook on Low for 8 to 10 hours; stir occasionally if possible.

Homemade Baked Beans

Ingredients

• ½ pound bacon

• 2 (14.5 ounce) cans Great Northern beans, rinsed and drained

• 2 small onions, chopped

• 1 cup water (Optional)

• ¾ cup packed brown sugar

• 3 tablespoons ketchup

• 3 tablespoons molasses

• 1 tablespoon vinegar

• 1 tablespoon mustard

• 1 teaspoon salt

• 1 teaspoon garlic powder

Directions

• Preheat the oven to 350 degrees F (175 degrees C). Grease a 2 1/2-quart baking dish.

• Place bacon in a large skillet and cook over medium-high heat until crisp, about 10 minutes; drain and cool on paper towels. Crumble bacon once cooled.

• Mix bacon, beans, onions, water, brown sugar, ketchup, molasses, vinegar, mustard, salt, and garlic powder together in the prepared baking dish. Cover the dish with aluminum foil.

• Bake in preheated oven until bubbling, 45 minutes.

Instant Pot Baked Beans

This Instant Pot baked beans recipe was passed down through my French Canadian family from my grandmother to my mother and then to me many years ago. It traditionally takes hours to make, as we let the beans slow cook overnight in the oven on low heat. I transformed it into a much quicker Instant Pot recipe with great success! With this method, you don't even have to presoak the beans. These are even better the next day and freeze well, too.

Ingredients

• 8 cups water

• 1 pound dry navy beans, rinsed and picked through

• 1 tablespoon olive oil

• 6 ounces salt pork, diced

• 6 ounces bacon, cut into small pieces

• 1 small onion, minced

• 1 ½ cups water, divided

• ⅓ cup molasses

• ¼ cup ketchup

• ¼ cup brown sugar

• 1 tablespoon yellow mustard

Directions

• Combine water and beans in a multi-functional pressure cooker (such as an Instant Pot). Close and lock the lid. Select high pressure according to manufacturer's instructions; set the timer for 15 minutes. Allow 10 to 15 minutes for pressure to build.

• Release pressure using the natural-release method according to manufacturer's instructions, about 20 minutes; quick-release remaining pressure according to manufacturer's directions. Unlock and remove the lid. Drain and rinse beans with cold water and set aside. Rinse and wipe out the Instant Pot insert and place back into the pressure cooker.

• Turn on the Instant Pot and select the Sauté function. Heat olive oil until shimmering, 2 to 3 minutes. Add salt pork, bacon, and onion; cook until fat begins to render, 1 to 2 minutes. Pour in 1/2 cup water and scrape any browned bits off the bottom. Turn the Instant Pot off.

• Whisk together molasses, ketchup, brown sugar, mustard, and remaining 1 cup water in a small bowl. Return cooked beans to the pot along with ketchup mixture. Gently stir to combine. Close and lock the lid. Select high pressure according to manufacturer's instructions; set the timer for 35 minutes. Allow 10 to 15 minutes for pressure to build.

• Release pressure using the natural-release method according to manufacturer's instructions, about 20 minutes; quick-release remaining pressure according to manufacturer's directions. Unlock and remove the lid. Beans will thicken as they cool. Serve immediately or freeze portions for later.

Tips

• The salt content of salt pork varies, so you may need to adjust the salt before serving.

• Older beans can take longer to cook, so you may need to increase cook time by 5 to 10 minutes if the beans are still firm.

Texas-Style Baked Beans

Take the time to make up a batch of these authentic Texas baked beans the next time you have an outdoor cookout. They are sure to be a hit! These are great if you don't have a smoker, but if you have access to a good hickory or pecan fire, take advantage.

Ingredients

• 1 tablespoon butter, or as needed

• 2 tablespoons vegetable oil

• 1 red onion, diced

• 2 cloves garlic, minced, or more to taste

• 1 tablespoon butter, or as needed

• 1 pound bacon, diced

• 1 red bell pepper, diced

• 3 jalapeno peppers, minced, or to taste

• 1 cup beer, or more to taste

• 1 cup barbeque sauce

• 1 cup brown sugar

• ¼ cup molasses

• 6 cups cooked pinto beans

• 1 pinch garlic salt, or to taste

• cracked black pepper to taste

Directions

• Preheat oven to 375 degrees F (190 degrees C). Grease a 9x13-inch baking dish with 1 tablespoon butter.

• Heat oil in a large skillet over medium-high heat. Saute onion and garlic in hot oil until onion begins to soften, 5 to 7 minutes. Add bacon, bell pepper, and jalapeno peppers; cook and stir until bacon is browned, 7 to 10 minutes more.

• Stir beer, barbeque sauce, brown sugar, and molasses together in a large bowl; add pinto beans and bacon mixture. Season with garlic salt and black pepper. Pour beans mixture into the prepared baking dish.

• Bake in the preheated oven until bubbling and browned, about 45 minutes.

Note:

• To bake beans on a wood smoker, preheat the smoker to between 250 degrees F (120 degrees C) and 275 degrees F (135 degrees C). Pour beans mixture into a greased 9x13-inch foil pan. Cook in the smoker for 30 minutes. Cover foil pan with aluminum foil and continue cooking for 2 to 3 hours. Remove aluminum foil cover and transfer beans to a preheated 375 degrees F (190 degrees C) oven for 10 minutes to brown the beans.

Baked Beans I

Ingredients

• 1 (29 ounce) can baked beans with pork

• ½ cup packed brown sugar

• ½ cup ketchup

• 1 tablespoon Worcestershire sauce

Directions

• Preheat oven to 350 degrees F (175 degrees C).

• In a casserole dish, combine beans, brown sugar, ketchup, and Worcestershire sauce.

• Bake, covered, for 45 minutes or until bubbly.

Better Baked Beans

Tangy, sweet old fashioned baked beans, are made the easy way in this side dish. This is my grandma's favorite semi home-made recipe. She makes it every Thanksgiving, and we usually end up scraping the pan clean! Never any leftovers!

Ingredients

• 2 (28 ounce) cans baked beans

• 1 small onion, chopped

• 2 tablespoons brown sugar

• 3 tablespoons pancake syrup

• 2 tablespoons ketchup

• 2 teaspoons prepared yellow mustard

• 4 slices bacon

Directions

• Preheat the oven to 350 degrees F (175 degrees C).

• In a large bowl, stir together the baked beans, onion, brown sugar, syrup, ketchup and mustard. Pour into a 9x13 inch baking dish, and lay strips of bacon across the top.

• Bake for 35 to 40 minutes in the preheated oven, until the bacon is browned and the beans have thickened.

Calico Bean Casserole

Kidney beans, baked beans and butter beans are combined with ground beef, bacon and onion and baked. It's thick, hearty, and pretty tasty too! This can also be done in a slow cooker.

Ingredients

• 1 (15 ounce) can kidney beans, undrained

• 1 (16 ounce) can baked beans with pork

• 1 (15 ounce) can butter beans, undrained

• ½ cup ketchup

• 2 teaspoons white vinegar

• 1 tablespoon dry mustard

• ¾ cup packed brown sugar

• 1 pound lean ground beef

• 4 ounces bacon, chopped

- ½ cup chopped onion

- salt to taste

- ground black pepper to taste

Directions

- Preheat oven to 350 degrees F (175 degrees C).

- In a large skillet over medium heat, fry the ground beef, bacon and onion together until ground beef is no longer pink. Drain fat.

- In a large mixing bowl, combine the kidney beans, baked beans with pork and butter beans. Stir in the ketchup, white vinegar, dry mustard, brown sugar and cook beef mixture. Mix thoroughly, adding salt and pepper to taste.

- Pour the bean and meat mixture into a 9x13 inch baking dish. Bake in preheated oven for 30 to 40 minutes.

Slow Cooker Baked Beans Using Canned Beans
Ingredients

- ½ cup hickory-flavored barbeque sauce

- ½ cup ketchup

- ½ cup packed brown sugar

- 1 teaspoon dry mustard

• 3 (14.5 ounce) cans great Northern beans, drained and rinsed

• 1 green bell pepper, diced

• 1 large onion, diced

• 4 ounces cooked ham, diced

Directions

• Mix barbeque sauce, ketchup, brown sugar, and mustard together in a 4-quart slow cooker until smooth. Stir beans, green bell pepper, onion, and ham into barbeque sauce mixture.

• Cook beans on Low for 8 to 12 hours until thick.

Note:

• The beans can also be cooked on High for 3 to 4 hours.

Bacon Baked Beans

Ingredients

• 6 slices bacon

• 2 (16 ounce) cans baked beans

• 1 onion, diced

• ¼ cup yellow mustard

• ¾ cup ketchup

• 1 cup packed brown sugar

• 1 Granny Smith apple - peeled, cored and diced

Directions

• Preheat the oven to 350 degrees F (175 degrees C). Cook bacon in a large skillet or in the microwave until much of the grease has been released, but the bacon is still flexible. Drain on paper towels and set aside.

• In a 9 inch square baking dish, stir together the baked beans, onion, mustard, ketchup, brown sugar and apple. Top with slices of bacon.

• Bake uncovered for 45 minutes in the preheated oven, until the bacon is crisp and beans are bubbling hot.

Slow Cooker Cowboy Beans

Ingredients

• 1 pound hamburger

• ½ pound bacon

• 1 (28 ounce) can baked beans with pork

• 1 (15 ounce) can kidney beans, rinsed and drained

• 1 (15 ounce) can lima beans, rinsed and drained

• 2 onions, chopped

• 1 cup ketchup

• 1 cup brown sugar

• 1 teaspoon prepared mustard

Directions

• Heat a large skillet over medium-high heat. Cook and stir hamburger and bacon together in the hot skillet until hamburger is browned and crumbly, 7 to 10 minutes.

• Stir cooked hamburger and bacon, baked beans with pork, kidney beans, lima beans, onions, ketchup, brown sugar, and mustard together in the bottom of your slow cooker.

• Cook on Low until hot and thickened, at least 3 hours.

Pat's Baked Beans

Ingredients

• 6 slices bacon

• 1 cup chopped onion

• 1 clove garlic, minced

• 1 (16 ounce) can pinto beans

• 1 (16 ounce) can great Northern beans, drained

• 1 (16 ounce) can baked beans

• 1 (16 ounce) can red kidney beans, drained

- 1 (15 ounce) can garbanzo beans, drained

- ¾ cup ketchup

- ½ cup molasses

- ¼ cup packed brown sugar

- 2 tablespoons Worcestershire sauce

- 1 tablespoon yellow mustard

- ½ teaspoon pepper

Directions

- Preheat oven to 375 degrees F (190 degrees C).

- Place bacon in a large, deep skillet. Cook over medium high heat until evenly brown. Drain, reserving 2 tablespoons of drippings, crumble and set aside in a large bowl. Cook the onion and garlic in the reserved drippings until onion is tender; drain excess grease and transfer to the bowl with the bacon.

- To the bacon and onions add pinto beans, northern beans, baked beans, kidney beans and garbanzo beans. Stir in ketchup, molasses, brown sugar, Worcestershire sauce, mustard and black pepper. Mix well and transfer to a 9x12 inch casserole dish.

- Cover and bake in preheated oven for 1 hour.

4-Bean Baked Beans

Ingredients

- 1 (15 ounce) can kidney beans, drained

- 1 (15 ounce) can butter beans, drained

- 1 (15 ounce) can lima beans, drained

- 1 (16 ounce) can pork and beans, drained

- ½ pound bacon, cut into small pieces

- 1 large onion, chopped

- 2 cloves garlic, chopped

- ¾ cup brown sugar

- ½ cup ketchup

- ½ cup vinegar

- ¼ cup molasses

- 1 teaspoon dry mustard

Directions

- Preheat oven to 350 degrees F (175 degrees C).

- Place kidney beans, butter beans, lima beans, and pork and beans in a 2-quart casserole dish.

• Heat a saucepan over medium heat; cook and stir bacon, onion, and garlic until bacon is browned, about 10 minutes. Pour off excess fat.

• Whisk brown sugar, ketchup, vinegar, molasses, and mustard into bacon mixture; simmer until cooked through, about 20 minutes. Pour sauce over beans in the casserole dish.

• Bake in the preheated oven until bubbling, 1 hour 15 minutes.

Spicy Baked Beans

Ingredients

• 4 slices bacon, or more to taste, cut into bite-size pieces

• 1 small onion, chopped

• 2 (28 ounce) cans baked beans

• ½ cup ketchup

• ½ cup brown sugar

• 2 tablespoons Worcestershire sauce

• 2 tablespoons prepared yellow mustard

• 2 tablespoons minced jalapeno pepper

• 1 tablespoon chili powder

• 1 tablespoon mustard powder

Directions

- Preheat oven to 350 degrees F (175 degrees C).

- Cook and stir bacon in a large skillet over medium-high heat to render some fat, 2 to 3 minutes. Stir onion into the rendered fat and cook until the bacon is crisp and the onion is tender, 7 to 10 minutes.

- Stir baked beans, ketchup, brown sugar, Worcestershire sauce, prepared mustard, minced jalapeno pepper, chili powder, and mustard powder together in a large bowl; add bacon mixture and stir. Pour the mixture into a 13x9-inch baking dish.

- Bake in the preheated oven until the liquid has thickened, 45 to 55 minutes

3BC (Best Baked Bean Casserole)

Ingredients

- 1 tablespoon butter

- 1 small onion, diced

- ½ pound bacon

- 1 (28 ounce) can baked beans (such as Bush's Original®)

- 2 teaspoons Worcestershire sauce

- 1 tablespoon ketchup

- 1 teaspoon prepared yellow mustard

• 1 cup brown sugar, divided

Directions

• Preheat an oven to 400 degrees F (200 degrees C).

• Melt the butter in a skillet over low heat. Cook and stir until the onion has softened and turned translucent, 10 to 15 minutes. Meanwhile, place the bacon in a large, deep skillet, and cook over medium-high heat, turning occasionally, until evenly browned, about 10 minutes. Drain the bacon slices on a paper towel-lined plate. Cut bacon into bite-sized pieces and set aside.

• Combine the baked beans, Worcestershire sauce, ketchup, mustard, and onions in a 2-quart casserole dish. Stir in 2/3 of the cooked bacon and 1/4 of the brown sugar until evenly mixed. Cover the bean mixture with the remaining bacon, and sprinkle with the remaining brown sugar.

• Bake in the preheated oven until hot and bubbly, about 45 minutes.

The Best Barbecue Baked Beans

It's not a real barbecue until a dish of baked beans shows up! While there are many different versions and many different techniques, I'm here to tell you that these are the best. These are the tastiest, most satisfying, the easiest, and the meatiest. They not only make a great side dish, but if the budget's a little tight, these will absolutely work as a main course. Sprinkle the top with sliced green onion if you like.

Ingredients

- 1 pound dried red beans

- 3 quarts water

- 1 bay leaf

- 1 ½ pounds boneless pork shoulder, cut into 2-inch cubes (Optional)

- 1 yellow onion, chopped

- 1 cup barbecue sauce

- ½ cup ketchup

- ⅓ cup apple cider vinegar

- ¼ cup packed light brown sugar

- 3 tablespoons molasses

- 2 tablespoons yellow mustard

- 1 teaspoon Worcestershire sauce

- 1 tablespoon smoked paprika

- ⅛ teaspoon cayenne pepper

• 1 teaspoon freshly ground black pepper

• 1 tablespoon kosher salt

• 1 teaspoon garlic powder

• 2 ½ cups reserved bean cooking liquid

• 6 slices thick-cut bacon

Directions

• Add dry beans to a bowl, cover with water, and let soak for 8 hours, or overnight.

• Drain beans and transfer to a large pot filled with 3 quarts of cold, fresh water. Add bay leaf, pork shoulder, and onion. Bring to a simmer over high heat. Reduce heat to medium-low and stir. Skim off foam if desired. Let simmer until beans are just tender, about 1 hour.

• While beans simmer, combine barbecue sauce, ketchup, vinegar, brown sugar, molasses, mustard, Worcestershire, smoked paprika, cayenne, black pepper, kosher salt, and garlic powder in a bowl with a whisk. Set aside until needed.

• Preheat the oven to 350 degrees F (175 degrees C).

• Transfer tender bean mixture to a deep, 15x10-inch baking dish using a spider strainer. Pour in barbecue sauce mixture and 2 ½ cups of the bean cooking liquid. Place bacon slices on top.

• Bake uncovered in the center of the preheated oven until the liquids have reduced into a thick sauce, 2 to 3 hours.

Notes:

• Any dry bean will work, but red beans are my recommendation.

• Baking time will depend on amount of liquid, as well as size and shape of pan, so start checking doneness after 1 1/2 hours, but may need to go much longer.

Boston Baked Beans

Ingredients

• 1 pound dry navy beans

• 6 cups water

• 1 pinch baking soda

• 1 bay leaf

• 6 slices bacon, cut into 1/2-inch pieces

• 1 yellow onion, diced

• ⅓ cup molasses

• ¼ cup packed dark brown sugar

• 1 teaspoon dry mustard powder

• 1 ½ teaspoons salt

• ½ teaspoon freshly ground black pepper, or to taste

Directions

• Soak navy beans overnight in a large bowl with enough water by several inches. Drain and place beans into a large Dutch oven or heavy pot with 6 cups water, baking soda, and bay leaf. Bring to a boil, reduce heat to medium, and boil for 10 minutes. Drain, saving bean-cooking liquid.

• Preheat oven to 300 degrees F (150 degrees C).

• Transfer beans into clean Dutch oven and stir bacon, onion, molasses, brown sugar, dry mustard, salt, and black pepper into beans. Pour enough of the hot reserved bean liquid in to cover beans; stir.

• Cover Dutch oven and bake in preheated oven for 1 hour. Check liquid level and add more of the reserved bean liquid to bring liquid up to cover beans. Return to oven and continue baking until beans are tender and almost all the liquid has been absorbed, about 1 hour.

• Raise oven heat to 350; bake beans uncovered in oven until top develops a flavorful crust, 20 to 30 more minutes.

Apple Baked Beans

Ingredients

• 4 (16 ounce) cans pork and beans

• 8 slices cooked bacon, crumbled

• 2 Granny Smith apples - peeled, cored, and diced

• 1 ⅓ cups barbeque sauce

• 1 cup brown sugar

• ¼ cup raisins (Optional)

Directions

• Preheat oven to 350 degrees F (175 degrees C).

• Stir pork and beans, bacon, apples, barbeque sauce, brown sugar, and raisins together in a 9x13-inch baking dish.

• Bake in preheated oven for 90 minutes.

Slow Cooker Baked Beans

Ingredients

• 1 pound dry great Northern beans

• 8 cups water

• 4 ounces diced salt pork

• 1 cup chopped onion

- ½ cup molasses

- ⅓ cup packed brown sugar

- 1 teaspoon dry mustard

- ⅛ teaspoon ground black pepper

Directions

• The night before, combine the Great Northern Beans and water in a large saucepan. Bring to a boil, and cook for 1 1/2 hours. Pour beans and their liquid into a bowl, cover and refrigerate overnight.

• In the morning, drain off liquid, reserving 1 cup. Pour beans and the reserved liquid into the crock of a slow cooker. Stir in the salt pork, onion, molasses, brown sugar, mustard and pepper. Cover, and cook on Low for 12 to 14 hours. Stir before serving.

Texas Cowboy Baked Beans

Ingredients

- 1 pound ground beef

- 4 (16 ounce) cans baked beans with pork

- 1 (4 ounce) can canned chopped green chile peppers

- 1 small Vidalia onion, peeled and chopped

- 1 cup barbeque sauce

• ½ cup brown sugar

• 1 tablespoon garlic powder

• 1 tablespoon chili powder

• 3 tablespoons hot pepper sauce (e.g. Tabasco), or to taste

Directions

• In a skillet over medium heat, brown the ground beef until no longer pink; drain fat, and set aside.

• In a 3 1/2 quart or larger slow cooker, combine the ground beef, baked beans, green chiles, onion and barbeque sauce. Season with brown sugar, garlic powder, chili powder and hot pepper sauce. Cook on HIGH for 2 hours, or low for 4 to 5 hours.

Slow Cooker Baked Beans with Ham Hock
Ingredients

• 24 ounces dry white beans

• 1 pound ham hocks

• 1 onion, chopped

• ½ cup packed brown sugar

• ½ cup maple syrup

• 1 teaspoon salt

• 1 cup water

• ½ cup ketchup

• 2 tablespoons prepared mustard

Directions

• In a large pot over high heat, combine the beans with water to cover and bring to a boil for 10 minutes. Remove from heat but let sit for 1 hour. Drain beans and place them in a slow cooker. Add the ham hocks, onion, brown sugar, maple syrup, salt and water.

• Mix well, cover and cook on high setting for 4 to 5 hours, stirring occasionally. During the final hour of cooking, add the ketchup and mustard, remove the ham from the hocks and discard the hocks. Mix well and serve.

Betty's 3-Bean Hot Dish (a la Minnesota)

Ingredients

• ¼ pound bacon

• 1 pound ground beef

• 1 onion, diced

• 1 (15 ounce) can pork and beans, drained

• 1 (15 ounce) can kidney beans, drained

• 1 (15 ounce) can butter beans, drained

• ½ cup ketchup

• ½ cup brown sugar

• 2 tablespoons white vinegar

• 1 tablespoon yellow mustard

Directions

• Place bacon in a large skillet and cook over medium-high heat, turning occasionally, until evenly browned, about 10 minutes. Drain bacon slices on paper towels. Crumble when cooled. Wipe out skillet with a paper towel.

• Cook and stir ground beef in the hot skillet until browned and crumbly, 5 to 7 minutes. Drain and discard grease. Add onion and cook until clear, about 5 minutes more.

• Combine cooked bacon, cooked beef, pork and beans, kidney beans, butter beans, ketchup, brown sugar, vinegar, and mustard in a slow cooker. Stir to combine. Cook on High until heated through, about 1 hour.

Note:

• To make this on the stovetop, add cooked meat and all other ingredients to a large skillet and simmer until heated through, about 15 minutes.

Ingredients

- 10 cups dried great Northern beans

- 1 pound salt pork

- 2 onions

- 2 ½ cups molasses

- 1 teaspoon black pepper

- 4 teaspoons dry hot mustard

- ½ cup butter

Directions

• The bean hole should be 2 1/2 to 3 feet deep, depending on your pot. The hole should be big enough around to have a 6 inch space between the pot and the edge of the hole on all sides. To help hold heat, put some old tire chains or stones in the hole before starting the fire.

• Start the fire and keep it filled with good dry hardwood. Let it burn for about 3 hours. The hole should be at least 3/4 full of hot coals. After the fire has been going for about an hour, place the beans in a large pot, on the stove with water to cover. Bring to a boil and cook until skins roll back when you blow on them, about 45 minutes. Watch closely, because they will get mushy if left too long.

• When the hole is ready, cut the salt pork in to 2 inch wide and 1/4 inch thick slices. Place them into the bottom of the bean pot. Peel and cut the onions in half; lay them on top of the pork. Pour the beans and their liquid into the pot, then mix in the molasses, black pepper and dry mustard. Slice butter and place on top. Add enough boiling water to cover the beans by one inch. Cover the top of the pot tightly with aluminum foil so that it goes down over the sides by at least 2 inches. Place lid onto bean pot.

• Before putting the pot into the hole, remove about 1/3 of the coals using a shovel. Remove and discard any burning pieces of wood. Place the bean pot into the hole, and put the coals from the hole back in around the sides and over the top of the bean pot. Now start filling the hole in with the dirt, packing it down with your feet as you go. You should end up with about 2 feet of dirt covering the pot. Cover the place where the beans are buried with a tarp or piece of metal to keep out rain.

• Let the beans stew overnight in their bean hole. Carefully dig them out the next day and enjoy!

Perfect BBQ Baked Beans
Ingredients

• 1 pound ground beef

• 1 small onion, minced

• 2 tablespoons dry mesquite flavored seasoning mix

• 2 (28 ounce) cans baked beans (such as Bush's Original®)

• ¼ cup molasses

• ¾ cup brown sugar

• ¾ cup barbeque sauce

• 2 teaspoons dry mustard powder

• 2 pinches cayenne pepper, or to taste (Optional)

Directions

• Preheat oven to 350 degrees F (175 degrees C).

• In a large skillet over medium heat, cook the ground beef, onion, and mesquite seasoning until the meat is no longer pink, breaking it up into crumbles as it cooks, about 10 minutes. Drain excess grease, and transfer the meat mixture to a large baking dish. Stir in the baked beans, molasses, brown sugar, barbeque sauce, dry mustard powder, and cayenne pepper, and mix until any small lumps of brown sugar have dissolved.

• Bake in the preheated oven until the beans are bubbling and the flavors have blended, about 20 minutes.

Down Home Baked Beans

Ingredients

- 1 pound bacon

- 2 (28 ounce) cans baked beans

- 1 (12 ounce) bottle chili sauce

- 1 large sweet onion, chopped

- 2 cups packed brown sugar

Directions

- Preheat oven to 350 degrees F (175 degrees C).

- Place bacon in a large, deep skillet. Cook over medium high heat until evenly brown. Drain, crumble and set aside.

- In a large bowl combine beans, chili sauce, onion, brown sugar and bacon. Pour into a 9x13 inch casserole dish.

- Bake in preheated oven for 45 minutes to 1 hour.

Bourbon and DP Baked Beans

Ingredients

- ½ cup brown sugar

- 1 tablespoon ground paprika

- 1 teaspoon dry mustard

- ¼ teaspoon cayenne pepper

- 1 (12 fl oz) can caffeinated pepper-type soda (such as Dr Pepper®)

- ¾ cup ketchup

- ¼ cup Worcestershire sauce

- 8 slices bacon

- 1 large onion, finely chopped

- 1 clove garlic, minced

- ¼ cup bourbon

- 2 (16 ounce) cans baked beans with pork

Directions

- Preheat oven to 350 degrees F (175 degrees C).

- Mix brown sugar, paprika, mustard, and cayenne pepper together in a bowl. Whisk in pepper soda, ketchup, and Worcestershire sauce until brown sugar is dissolved.

- Cut 4 slices of bacon into small strips. Cook and stir in a large Dutch oven over medium heat until almost crispy, 3 to 5 minutes. Transfer to a bowl, reserving bacon grease.

- Stir onion into the bacon grease in the Dutch oven; cook and stir until soft, 3 to 5 minutes. Add garlic; cook and stir for 1 minute.

Pour in bourbon, stirring to scrape up browned bits off the bottom with a wooden spoon. Stir bacon strips back in.

• Pour brown sugar mixture and baked beans into the Dutch oven. Simmer until beans are heated through, about 15 minutes. Arrange remaining 4 slices of bacon on top of the beans.

• Bake in the preheated oven, covered, until beans are bubbly and sauce is syrupy, about 3 hours.

Quick Instant Pot Baked Beans

Ingredients

• 8 slices bacon, chopped

• 2 (15 ounce) cans baked beans with pork

• ½ cup ketchup

• 6 tablespoons brown sugar

• ½ teaspoon dry mustard powder

Directions

• Turn on a multi-functional pressure cooker (such as Instant Pot®) and select Saute function. Add bacon and cook until browned and crispy but not burned, about 6 minutes. Transfer bacon to a baking sheet lined with paper towels. Allow grease to drain.

• Pour off some liquid from the beans, clearing at least 1 inch from the top of the can, but leaving some liquid. Add beans and remaining liquid, ketchup, brown sugar, and mustard to the Instant Pot®. Mix in bacon. Close and lock the lid. Select high pressure according to manufacturer's instructions; set timer for 3 minutes. Allow 10 to 15 minutes for pressure to build.

• Release pressure carefully using the quick-release method according to manufacturer's instructions, about 5 minutes. Unlock and remove the lid.

Baked Beans with Beef

Ingredients

• 1 pound ground beef

• 1 large onion, finely chopped

• 1 pound peppered bacon

• 7 (28 ounce) cans baked beans (such as Bush's® Original)

• 1 (15 ounce) can black beans, drained

• 1 (15 ounce) can light red kidney beans, drained

• 1 (15 ounce) can dark red kidney beans, drained

• 1 (15 ounce) can great northern beans, drained

• ½ cup brown sugar

- ¼ cup prepared yellow mustard

- ¼ cup soy sauce

Directions

- Heat a large skillet over medium-high heat. Add ground beef and onion. Cook and stir until beef is browned and crumbly, 5 to 7 minutes. Drain and discard grease. Transfer beef to the slow cooker.

- Place bacon in the skillet and cook over medium-high heat, turning occasionally, until evenly browned, about 10 minutes. Drain bacon slices on paper towels. Crumble into small pieces and add to the slow cooker.

- Add baked beans, black beans, light and dark kidney beans, great northern beans, sugar, mustard, and soy sauce to the slow cooker; mix well with beef and bacon.

- Cook on Medium until flavors meld, about 4 hours.

Simple Baked Beans II

Ingredients

- ½ pound bacon, chopped

- 1 onion, finely chopped

- 2 (15 ounce) cans baked beans

- ¼ cup brown sugar

• ¼ cup ketchup

• ¼ cup prepared mustard

Directions

• Place bacon in a large, deep skillet. Cook over medium high heat until evenly brown. Add the onion and saute until tender. Drain excess oil, if desired. Stir in the beans, brown sugar, ketchup and mustard. Cook, stirring occasionally, until bubbly.

Simple Slow Cooker Pinto Beans and Ham

Ingredients

• 14 cups water, divided

• 2 cups dried pinto beans

• 1 ham bone with meat

• 1 large red onion, chopped

• 2 teaspoons garlic, minced

• 1 teaspoon ham base (such as Better than Bouillon)

• 1 dash hot pepper sauce (such as Tabasco), or to taste

• 1 pinch salt and ground black pepper to taste

Directions

• Bring 8 cups water and pinto beans to a boil in a large pot. Remove pot from heat, cover, and let stand for 1 hour. Drain and rinse before using.

• Transfer pinto beans to a slow cooker. Add ham bone, red onion, minced garlic, and ham base. Pour in remaining 6 cups of water, or enough to cover the beans.

• Cool on Low until beans are tender, about 8 hours.

• Remove the ham bone, shred meat, and add back to the beans. Discard the bone. Serve hot, seasoned with hot sauce, salt, and pepper.

Note:

• I usually follow the quick-soak method instructions on the pinto bean package for expediency, but if you prefer to soak overnight, then follow that method.

Easy Baked Beans

Ingredients

• cooking spray

• 2 (16 ounce) cans pork and beans

• ¾ cup brown sugar

• ¼ cup ketchup

• ¼ cup barbeque sauce

• 4 slices bacon, cut into 1/2-inch pieces

• 1 teaspoon dry mustard

Directions

• Preheat oven to 325 degrees F (165 degrees C). Prepare a 9-inch baking dish with cooking spray.

• Stir pork and beans, brown sugar, ketchup, barbeque sauce, bacon, and dry mustard together in the prepared baking dish.

• Bake in preheated oven, stirring every 20 minutes or so, until bacon fat is rendered throughout the beans mixture, 2 1/4 to 2 1/2 hours.

Skillet Baked Beans

Ingredients

• 6 slices bacon, cut into 1-inch pieces

• 4 (16 ounce) cans pork and beans

• 1 cup chopped onion

• ½ cup packed brown sugar

• 6 tablespoons molasses

• 2 teaspoons yellow mustard

Directions

• Cook and stir bacon in a large skillet over medium-high heat until crisp, about 10 minutes.

• Stir pork and beans, onion, brown sugar, molasses, and mustard with bacon in the skillet; bring to a boil, reduce heat to medium-low, and simmer, stirring occasionally, until thickened, 15 to 20 minutes.

Gigantes (Greek Lima Beans)

Ingredients

• 1 (16 ounce) package dried lima beans

• 2 (16 ounce) cans chopped tomatoes with juice

• 1 cup olive oil

• 3 cloves garlic, chopped

• 1 teaspoon chopped fresh dill

• sea salt to taste

• 1 cup water, or as needed (Optional)

Directions

• Place lima beans into a large saucepan and add enough water to cover by 2 inches. Soak for 8 hours or overnight.

• When ready to cook, preheat the oven to 375 degrees F (190 degrees C).

• Place the saucepan with beans and water over medium heat and bring to a boil. Reduce the heat to medium-low and simmer for 20 minutes.

• Drain beans; pour into a 9x13-inch baking dish. Add tomatoes, olive oil, garlic, dill, and salt; stir to combine.

• Bake in the preheated oven, stirring occasionally and adding water if the mixture appears dry, until beans are tender, 1 1/2 to 2 hours.

Tips

• You can substitute 2 teaspoons parsley for the dill if preferred.

Old Fashioned Baked Beans

Ingredients

• 10 cups water

• 2 cups dried navy beans

• 8 slices crisply cooked bacon, crumbled

• ½ cup chopped onion

• ½ cup packed brown sugar

• ¼ cup molasses

• 1 teaspoon salt

• 3 cups water

Directions

• Bring 10 cups water and navy beans to a boil in a large pot; cook at a boil for 2 minutes. Stir bacon, onion, brown sugar, molasses, and salt into the water.

• Carefully pour the mixture into a slow cooker.

• Cook on High, stirring occasionally, for 4 hours.

• Stir 3 cups water into the mixture. Continue cooking until beans are tender, about 2 hours 15 minutes more.

Rancho Baked Beans

Ingredients

• 1 pound ground beef

• 2 cups chopped onion

• 2 (16 ounce) cans pork and beans

• 1 (16 ounce) can kidney beans, drained

• 1 cup ketchup

• ¾ cup brown sugar

• 2 tablespoons mustard

• 1 tablespoon white vinegar

• 1 teaspoon salt

Directions

• Preheat oven to 350 degrees F (175 degrees C). Spray a casserole dish with cooking spray.

• Cook and stir ground beef and onion in a skillet over medium heat until beef is browned and onions are translucent, 10 to 15 minutes. Drain well.

• Mix pork and beans, kidney beans, ketchup, brown sugar, mustard, vinegar, and salt in a large bowl. Stir hamburger mixture into bean mixture. Pour hamburger-bean mixture into prepared casserole dish.

• Bake in the preheated oven until bubbling, about 45 minutes.

Loaded Baked Beans

Ingredients

• 8 slices bacon, coarsely chopped

• 1 small onion, chopped

• 1 green bell pepper, chopped

• 1 (16 ounce) can B&M® Original Baked Beans

• 1 (15.5 ounce) can Joan of Arc® Dark Red Kidney Beans

• 1 (15 ounce) can Joan of Arc® Spicy Chili Beans

• ½ cup BBQ sauce

• ½ cup shredded Cheddar cheese

• 2 green onions, chopped

Directions

• Preheat oven to 375 degrees F. Cook bacon in large nonstick skillet until crisp. Remove bacon to paper towel. Remove all but 3 tablespoons bacon fat. Add onion and pepper and cook 5 minutes or until softened.

• Add beans, BBQ sauce, and half the bacon and bring to a boil.

• Transfer beans to 1 1/2-quart baking dish. Cover with aluminum foil and bake 20 minutes or until bubbling.

• Remove foil and top with cheese and reserved bacon. Bake 5 minutes or until cheese is melted.

• Sprinkle with green onion.

Sweet Barbeque Beans

Ingredients

• 6 slices bacon, chopped

• 1 pound ground beef

• 2 (16 ounce) cans baked beans with pork

• 1 (15.5 ounce) can navy beans, rinsed and drained

- 1 (15 ounce) can kidney beans, rinsed and drained

- ¾ cup ketchup

- ¾ cup packed brown sugar

- 3 tablespoons distilled white vinegar

- 2 tablespoons honey garlic sauce

- 2 tablespoons sweet and sour sauce

- 1 teaspoon onion powder

- 1 teaspoon garlic salt

- 1 teaspoon ground mustard

- 1 teaspoon Worcestershire sauce

Directions

- Fry the bacon pieces in a large skillet until browned and crisp, remove from the pan and set aside. Crumble the ground beef into the pan; cook and stir until no longer pink, then drain off grease. Transfer the ground beef and bacon to a slow cooker.

- Pour the baked beans, navy beans, kidney beans, ketchup, brown sugar and vinegar into the slow cooker. Season with honey garlic sauce, sweet and sour sauce, onion powder, garlic salt, mustard powder and Worcestershire sauce. Stir until everything is distributed evenly. Cover, and cook on High heat for 1 hour before serving.

Ingredients

- 2 (15 ounce) cans pork and beans

- 1 (16 ounce) can kidney beans, rinsed and drained

- 1 (15 ounce) can lima beans, rinsed and drained

- 1 onion, chopped

- ½ cup packed brown sugar

- ½ cup ketchup

- ½ teaspoon dry mustard

- 4 strips cooked bacon, crumbled

Directions

- Preheat oven to 350 degrees F (175 degrees C). Grease a 2 1/2-quart baking dish.

- Combine pork and beans, kidney beans, lima beans, onion, brown sugar, ketchup, and dry mustard together in a bowl; transfer to the prepared baking dish. Sprinkle bacon over bean mixture. Cover dish with aluminum foil.

- Bake in the preheated oven for 30 minutes. Remove aluminum foil and continue baking until bubbling, about 30 minutes more.

Note:

• Butter beans can be substituted for the lima beans.

Erika's Baked Beans

Ingredients

• 4 slices bacon

• 1 (16 ounce) can pork and beans

• ½ cup chopped onion

• 2 tablespoons brown sugar, or more to taste

• 1 tablespoon Worcestershire sauce

• 1 teaspoon prepared mustard

Directions

• Preheat oven to 350 degrees F (175 degrees C).

• Place bacon in a large skillet and cook over medium-high heat, turning occasionally, until evenly browned, about 10 minutes. Drain the bacon slices on paper towels.

• Combine pork and beans, onion, brown sugar, Worcestershire sauce, and mustard in a 2-quart casserole dish. Chop drained bacon and stir into pork and beans mixture. Cover dish with aluminum foil.

• Bake in preheated oven for 90 minutes.

Ingredients

- 1 (16 ounce) package dried navy beans

- water as needed

- 2 cups chopped sweet onion

- ¼ cup firmly packed brown sugar

- ¼ cup molasses

- 2 tablespoons cider vinegar

- 2 teaspoons dry mustard

- 1 clove garlic, minced

- ¼ teaspoon ground nutmeg

- ¼ teaspoon ground cinnamon

- ¼ teaspoon ground black pepper

Directions

- Place navy beans into a large container and cover with several inches of cool water; let stand 8 hours to overnight.

- Drain navy beans and put into a pot with 5 cups water.

- Bring water to a boil; reduce heat and simmer until beans are tender, about 1 hour.

• Preheat oven to 250 degrees F (120 degrees C).

• Combine beans, onion, brown sugar, molasses, vinegar, mustard, garlic, nutmeg, and cinnamon in a 2-quart casserole dish with a lid; season with pepper. Place lid on dish.

• Bake in the preheated oven, 5 to 7 hours, stirring halfway through and adding water if mixture is too dry. Remove lid and bake until mixture has reduced to desired thickness, about 1 hour more.

Note:

• Vegetable broth can be substituted for the water.

Baked Meaty Beans

Ingredients

• 1 pound thick cut bacon

• 1 pound lean ground beef

• ½ pound sage pork sausage

• 1 clove garlic, crushed

• 1 large onion, cut into 1/2-inch pieces

• 1 cup dark brown sugar

• 1 cup real maple syrup

• 1 cup ketchup

- ¼ cup prepared yellow mustard

- ½ cup chipotle sauce

- 1 (16 ounce) can baked beans

- 1 (16 ounce) can kidney beans

- 1 (16 ounce) can black beans

- 1 (16 ounce) can pinto beans

- 1 (16 ounce) can great Northern beans

- 1 (16 ounce) can cannellini beans

- 1 tablespoon chili powder

- salt to taste

Directions

- Place bacon in a Dutch oven over medium-high heat and cook until evenly brown. Drain, crumble and set aside.

- Place beef, sausage and garlic in Dutch oven and cook over medium-high heat until well done. Drain grease. Mix in onion and cook until tender. Stir in brown sugar, syrup, ketchup, mustard and chipotle sauce. Reduce heat to medium-low. Bring to a boil and cook 20 minutes, stirring often.

• Mix bacon, baked beans, kidney beans, black beans, pinto beans, great Northern beans and cannellini beans into Dutch oven. Continue cooking 20 minutes.

• Preheat oven to 350 degrees F (175 degrees C). Line a baking sheet with aluminum foil. Season beans with chili powder and salt.

• Place Dutch oven on prepared baking sheet on lowest rack of preheated oven. Bake 30 minutes. Let stand 10 minutes before serving.

Western-Style Baked Beans

Ingredients

• 1 pound ground beef

• 2 (28 ounce) cans baked beans with pork

• 1 pound bacon, cooked and crumbled

• ½ pound cooked ham, chopped

• 2 tablespoons minced onion

• 1 tablespoon chili powder

• ¼ cup ketchup

• ¼ cup packed brown sugar

• 1 tablespoon molasses

• ¼ cup water (Optional)

Directions

• Crumble the ground beef in a large skillet over medium-high heat. Cook and stir until no longer pink, 5 to 10 minutes. Drain off grease and transfer the beef to a 4 quart or larger slow cooker. Stir in the baked beans, bacon, ham, onion, chili powder, ketchup, brown sugar and molasses. If it seems thick, stir in the water. Cover and cook on High for 3 hours or cook for 6 to 8 hours on Low.

Kansas Baked Beans

Ingredients

• ½ pound bacon, diced

• ½ pound ground beef

• 1 onion, diced

• ½ cup white sugar

• ½ cup brown sugar

• ¼ cup ketchup

• ¼ cup barbeque sauce

• 2 tablespoons prepared yellow mustard

• 2 tablespoons molasses

- 2 teaspoons chili powder

- ½ teaspoon ground black pepper

- 1 (16 ounce) can kidney beans, rinsed and drained

- 1 (16 ounce) can butter beans, rinsed and drained

- 2 (16 ounce) cans pork and beans

Directions

- Preheat an oven to 350 degrees F (175 degrees C).

- Heat a skillet over medium heat. Cook the bacon, ground beef, and onion in the skillet until the bacon and ground beef are completely browned, 7 to 10 minutes. Drain any excess fat, and transfer to a casserole dish.

- Stir the white sugar, brown sugar, ketchup, barbeque sauce, mustard, molasses, chili powder, and black pepper together in a bowl; pour over the bacon mixture. Add the kidney beans, butter beans, and pork and beans; mix thoroughly.

- Bake in the preheated oven until the liquid thickens, about 1 hour.

Vegetarian Baked Beans with Canned Beans

Ingredients

- 2 teaspoons vegetable oil

- 1 medium onion, chopped

• 1 jalapeno pepper, seeded and diced

• 1 tablespoon minced garlic

• ¼ cup bourbon

• ⅓ cup tomato paste

• ¼ cup maple syrup

• 2 tablespoons molasses

• 2 tablespoons apple cider vinegar

• 2 tablespoons soy sauce

• 2 tablespoons yellow mustard

• 1 teaspoon smoked paprika

• 2 (15 ounce) cans navy beans, rinsed and drained

Directions

• Preheat the oven to 350 degrees F (175 degrees C).

• Heat oil in a large skillet over medium-high heat. Add onion and jalapeno. Cook until onion is soft and translucent, about 5 minutes. Add garlic and cook for 1 minute. Add bourbon and simmer for 4 minutes. Turn heat off.

• Combine tomato paste, maple syrup, molasses, vinegar, soy sauce, mustard, and paprika in a large bowl; whisk until smooth. Add onion mixture and beans; gently stir to combine.

• Transfer to a baking dish. Cover and cook for 35 minutes. Uncover and cook for 15 more minutes. Remove from the oven and let sit for 5 minutes before serving.

Bar-B-Q Baked Beans
Ingredients

• 1 (15 ounce) can kidney beans, drained (Optional)

• 1 (15 ounce) can pinto beans, drained

• 1 (15 ounce) can lima beans, drained

• 1 (16 ounce) can great Northern beans, drained

• 1 (12 ounce) bottle chili sauce

• 2 tablespoons brown sugar

• 1 tablespoon Dijon mustard

• 1 tablespoon Worcestershire sauce

• 2 tablespoons molasses

• 3 slices bacon, cut in half

Directions

• Preheat oven to 325 degrees F (165 degrees C).

• In a medium baking dish, mix kidney beans, pinto beans, lima beans, great northern beans, chili sauce, brown sugar, Dijon mustard, Worcestershire sauce and molasses. Top with bacon.

• Bake 1 hour in the preheated oven, until thick and bubbly.

Chuckwagon Beans
Ingredients

• ½ pound bacon, cut into small pieces

• 1 onion, cut into small pieces

• 2 (15 ounce) cans kidney beans, rinsed and drained

• ½ cup ketchup

• ½ teaspoon dry mustard

• 2 tablespoons brown sugar

• 1 tablespoon Worcestershire sauce

• 1 dash hot pepper sauce (such as Tabasco®)

• 1 pinch salt

• 1 pinch ground black pepper

Directions

• Preheat oven to 350 degrees F (175 degrees C).

• Heat a large pot over medium-high heat. Cook and stir bacon and onion in pot until the onion is tender, 7 to 10 minutes; add ketchup, dry mustard, brown sugar, Worcestershire sauce, hot pepper sauce, salt, and black pepper.

• Reduce heat to low and cook bean mixture at a simmer until hot, about 10 minutes; pour into a large casserole dish.

• Bake in preheated oven until bubbling on top, 10 to 15 minutes.

Ranch Beans with Beef

Ingredients

• 1 pound ground beef

• 3 (14.5 ounce) cans pork and beans, drained

• 1 cup ketchup

• 1 cup brown sugar

• ½ cup cold water

• ¼ cup distilled white vinegar

• 2 tablespoons mustard

Directions

• Preheat oven to 350 degrees F (175 degrees C). Grease a 13x9-inch baking dish.

• Heat a large skillet over medium-high heat. Cook and stir beef in the hot skillet until browned and crumbly, 5 to 7 minutes; drain and discard grease.

• Mix browned beef, pork and beans, cold water, white vinegar, and mustard together in the prepared baking dish.

• Bake in preheated oven until beginning to dry around the edges, about 1 hour.